Chen and the Pink Pot

by Janice Pimm

Illustrated by Pham Hoang Giang

OXFORD

UNIVERSITY PRESS

Long, long ago …

The Emperor of China stood on his balcony and sighed. He was <u>often</u> sad because he was getting old and he had no children. There was no one to be emperor after him.

One day, he had a bright idea. "I will have a competition. I will ask every child to grow a plant. The winner will be emperor after me."

The emperor was <u>often</u> sad. Does this mean he was sad a lot of the time or not much of the time?

Children from all over China travelled to the emperor's palace.

The emperor gave each child a pot and a seed.

"Go home and plant your seed in your pot," the emperor said. "Then bring your pots back to the palace. I will <u>choose</u> the winner."

How is the emperor going to <u>choose</u> the winner? What do you think the children have to do to win his competition?

Chen got a pink pot.
Then he got a pip.

I will put it in the pot.

child

Chen carried his pot home. Then he carefully planted his seed. He watered it every day, but his seed didn't grow.

"There isn't even one green shoot!" Chen said, unhappily.

Even so, he didn't give up.

The day came to return to the emperor's palace. Chen's friend, Yu Yan, arrived at his home. Her pot contained a beautiful rose bush.

"Come on! We must set off!" Yu Yan cried, hurrying out of the house. "We have a great distance to travel."

Chen followed her with his empty pot, feeling sad.

child

Chen, we must go.

9

Children arrived at the palace with huge plants, small plants, tall plants, thin plants and thick plants. Some children had flowering plants and some even had small trees!

Only Chen's pot was empty.

The emperor stared at the plants. Then he roared in a <u>fierce</u> voice, "Every <u>single</u> one of you has cheated! I gave you old seeds that would not grow. I wanted to find an honest child!"

Just then, the emperor spotted Chen's pink pot.

The emperor spoke in a <u>fierce</u> voice. Can you sound like the emperor and speak in a <u>fierce</u> voice?

Bring me the pink pot. Be quick!

Has every <u>single</u> child cheated, like the emperor thinks? Who is the <u>single</u> child who was honest?

"You are the only honest child here," the emperor said, smiling at Chen. "You will live in my palace and be emperor after me."

Answer the questions

1 What colour was Chen's pot?

green	pink

2 What did Chen do with his seed?

He watered it every day.	He put it in the shade.

3 What did Yu Yan grow?

a lemon tree	a rose bush

4 Why did the emperor choose Chen as the winner?

He grew the biggest plant.	He was honest.